FOR KIJANA, NIALAH & YOKI

Peace & Blessings
Alile

TEXT COPYRIGHT © 1989 ALILE SHARON LARKIN
PICTURES COPYRIGHT © 1992 ALILE SHARON LARKIN
COPYRIGHT © 2018 ALILE SHARON LARKIN

ALL RIGHTS RESERVED. THIS BOOK, OR PARTS THEREOF, MAY NOT BE REPRODUCED IN ANY FORM WITHOUT PERMISSION IN WRITING FROM THE PUBLISHER. DREADLOCKS AND THE THREE BEARS PRODUCTIONS. 3651 S. LA BREA AVE. #1015, LOS ANGELES, CALIFORNIA 90016. THE SCANNING, UPLOADING AND DISTRIBUTION OF THIS BOOK VIA THE INTERNET OR VIA ANY OTHER MEANS WITHOUT THE PERMISSION OF THE PUBLISHER IS ILLEGAL AND PUNISHABLE BY LAW. PLEASE PURCHASE ONLY AUTHORIZED ELECTRONIC EDITIONS, AND DO NOT PARTICIPATE IN OR ENCOURAGE ELECTRONIC PIRACY OF COPYRIGHTED MATERIALS. YOUR SUPPORT OF THE AUTHOR'S RIGHTS IS APPRECIATED. THE PUBLISHER DOES NOT HAVE ANY CONTROL OVER AND DOES NOT ASSUME ANY RESPONSIBILITY FOR AUTHOR OR THIRD-PARTY WEBSITES OR CONTENT.

FIRST EDITION 2018

ORIGINAL ILLUSTRATIONS WERE HAND DRAWN, THEN COLLAGED WITH CONSTRUCTION PAPER AND WALLPAPER.

PRODUCTION COORDINATOR/COVER DESIGN   JOM KIJANA RIVERS
BOOK DESIGN/HAND LETTERING   SIMON ESTRADA

DREADLOCKS AND THE THREE BEARS

ALILE SHARON LARKIN

DREADLOCKS AND THE THREE BEARS PRODUCTIONS
LOS ANGELES, CALIFORNIA

Not so far away from here on an island in the Caribbean lived a Cinnamon brown girl named Neenee. She had lots and lots of African curls on her pretty little Cinnamon brown head.

Neenee had curly curly, kinky curly, nappy curly twists and locks of hair called dreadlocks. Neenee's hair was so simply divine that everyone just called her Dreadlocks.

Everybody knew everybody else in her island village.

No one locked doors because they were all *friends* and *relations*.

Dreadlocks had one relation, her Auntie Samella who moved not so far away to America. Auntie Samella loved cuddly teddy bears so much that she ran off to live in the Teddy Bear Forest.

Everyone knows that is the home of the *Three Bear*.

Auntie Samella was a carpenter. She lived there happily repairing bear furniture and homes. She really missed her favorite niece Dreadlocks and so one summer she sent for her.

8

Dreadlocks rode in a boat. an *airplane*...

a car...
and a bus to the Teddy Bear Forest.

Even though Dreadlocks was happy to be with Auntie Samella again, she just couldn't wait to meet those bears.

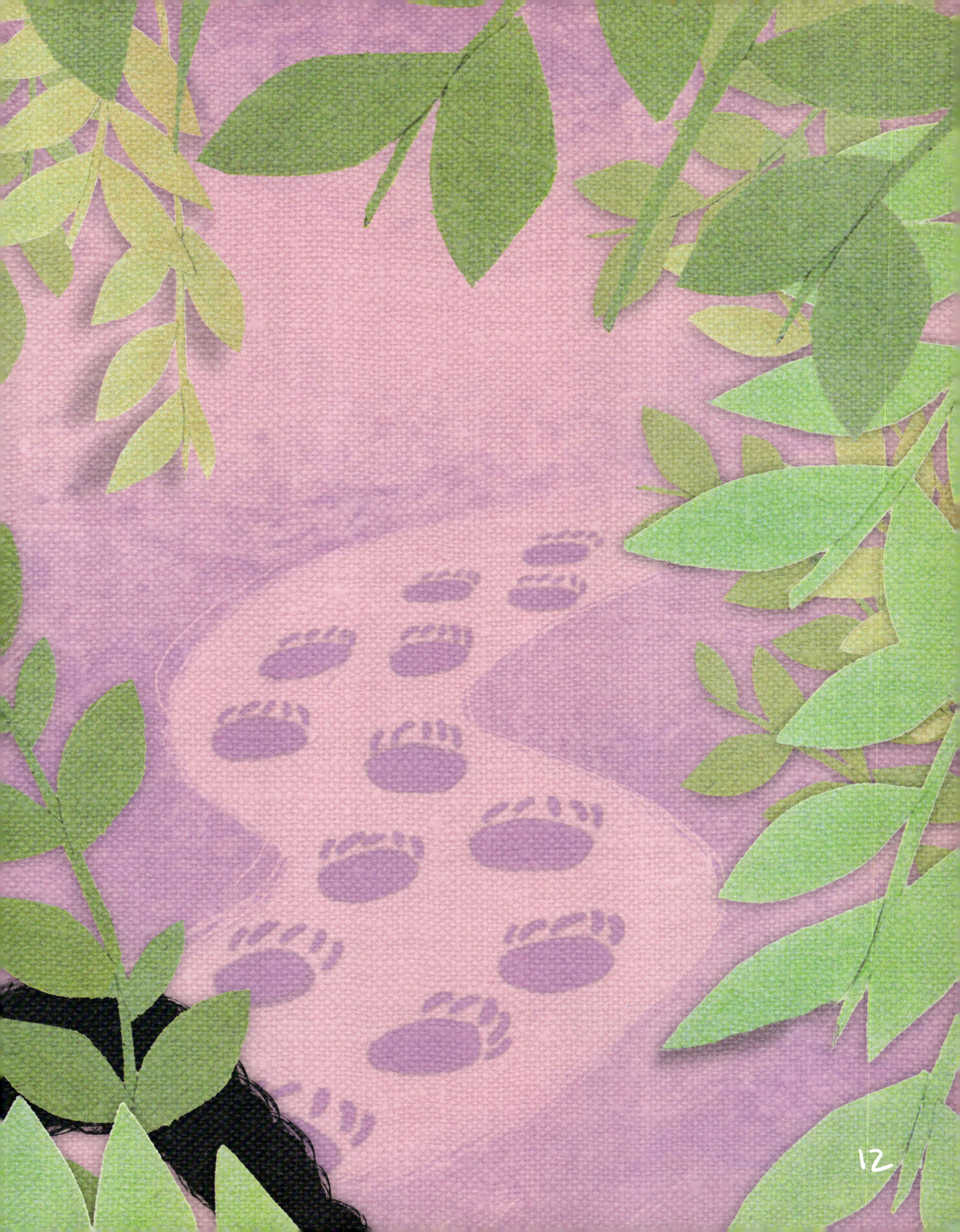

Before Auntie Samella had a chance to properly introduce them, Dreadlocks decided to find the Three Bears' house on her own.

Meanwhile at The Three Bears' house, Baby Boy Bear was just waking up.
"Daddy won't you please fix me some of your simply delicious cheese grits?" asked Baby Boy Bear with a sleepy groggy little bitty voice.

Daddy Bear said, "Yes," and he did. Oh those grits smelled wonderful. But there were problems.

Daddy Bear's simply delicious cheese grits were too hot, much too hot. Mama Bear suggested that they all take a nice morning walk to the pond while the grits cooled. As soon as the three of them disappeared down the road, Dreadlocks reached their house.

Now no one locks doors in The Teddy Bear Forest, just like in Dreadlocks' little island village. She felt right at home poking one foot inside their doorway, then poking her whole head through the dooway, where of course she smelled the grits! Daddy Bear's simply delicious grits smelled simply divine and next to teddy bears and Auntie Samella and her family and friends back home in her island village, there was nothing in the world that Dreadlocks loved better than cheese grits.

Dreadlocks saw three bowls on the table — Daddy Bear's great big bowl, Mama Bear's medium size bowl and Baby Boy Bear's little bitty bowl.

18

She picked up Daddy Bear's great big spoon and took a great big spoonful out of his great big bowl.
"Oh no," she said, "much too hot!"
She picked up Mama Bear's medium size spoon and took a medium size spoonful out of Mama Bear's medium size bowl.
"Oh no," she said, "much too cold."

19

Then she took Baby Boy Bear's little bitty spoon and took a little bitty spoonful out of his little bitty bowl. "Oh yes," she said, "just right."
She ate Baby Boy Bear's grits all up.

Dreadlocks was full of simply delicious cheese grits. She decided to sit a bit. There were three chairs in front of the fireplace — a great big chair, a medium size chair and a little bitty chair. Dreadlocks plopped down in the great big chair. "Ouch!" she said. It was too hard.

She sat down on the medium size chair but it was so soft she felt like she was sinking.

She sat down on the little bitty chair.
It was just right. "Ah," she sighed.
Now besides cheese grits, teddy bears, Auntie Samella
and her family and friends back home in her little
island village, there was nothing in the world that
Dreadlocks loved more than rocking in a rocking chair.
Dreadlocks started rocking. She rocked and rocked and
rocked and rocked and rocked. Dreadlocks rocked in that rocking
chair until it just fell apart.

23

Dreadlocks felt so bad about breaking the chair that she started to cry. She went upstairs to lie down and figure things out. There were three beds — a great big bed, a medium size bed and a little bitty bed. Dreadlocks tried all three.

The great big bed was too hard.

The medium size bed was too soft.

...but that little bitty bed was just right. Dreadlocks fell fast asleep.

Soon after she fell asleep, the three bears came home. Mama Bear knew right away that something was wrong. Baby Boy Bear ran to the table to eat his grits when Daddy Bear growled, "Somebody's been eating my cheese grits!"

Mama Bear hurried to check her bowl. "Oh!" she shouted, "Somebody's been eating my cheese grits too!"

Baby Boy Bear sobbed into his empty bowl, "Somebody's been eating my cheese grits and ate them all up!"

The Three Bears saw a pile of sticks by the fireplace and hurried to their chairs. Daddy Bear growled, "Somebody's been sitting in my chair." Mama Bear shouted, "Somebody's been sitting in my chair too!" By this time Baby Boy Bear knew that the pile of sticks was his chair. "Somebody's been sitting in my chair and broke it to pieces," he cried.

The three bears ran upstairs. Daddy Bear saw his bed all messed up, the covers half way on the floor and he growled, "Somebody's been sleeping in my bed."

Mama Bear, very upset about somebody going through all her family's things, saw her fancy pillows scattered all over the bed. Mama Bear shouted, "Somebody's been sleeping in my bed too!"

Then Baby Boy Bear saw a small cinnamon brown lump of little girl with the pretty pretty African curls sound asleep on his bed. Baby Boy Bear shouted, "Somebody's still sleeping in my bed! HERE SHE IS!" He yelled right into Dreadlocks' ears and scared her wide awake.

"Don't be frightened," he said. "I'm Baby Boy Bear. You must be Dreadlocks. Auntie Samella told us all about you. This is my mama and this is my daddy."

Dreadlocks said, "I'm sorry for eating all your grits and breaking your rocking chair. Listen, I make a pretty good pot of cheese grits myself and I know y'all know my Auntie Samella."

"Your Auntie Samella is the best carpenter in Teddy Bear Forest!" shouted the bears.

33

Dreadlocks gave Baby Boy Bear a hug and said, "We'll make everything as good as new."

So Dreadlocks cooked up some of her simply delicious cheese grits. Auntie Samella hammered and nailed Baby Boy Bear's rocking chair back together, even better than before. Then they all sat down together and ate lots and lots of Dreadlock's simply delicious cheese grits.

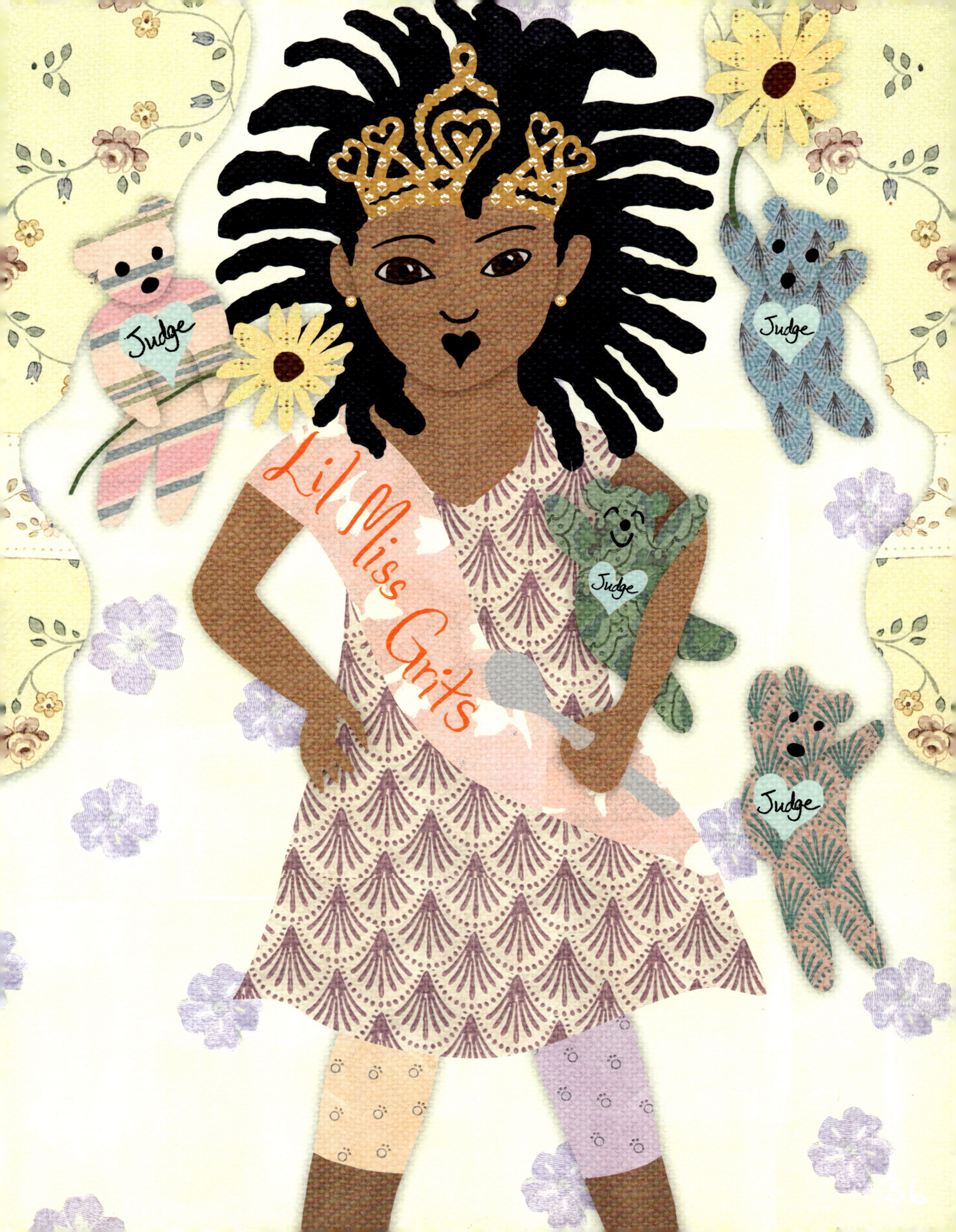
Judge
Lil Miss Grits
Judge
Judge
Judge

About the Author

Alile Sharon Larkin is an award-winning multicultural artist-educator and L.A. Rebellion filmmaker. Larkin was a public school teacher for over twenty-five years with the Los Angeles Unified School District. She received ten KLCS/PBS Video-in-the Classroom awards for teacher-produced videos documenting student learning about textile arts, storytelling, yoga, jazz, women's history, Kwanzaa and African-inspired dance. She especially loved teaching children to write and illustrate their very own picture books as documented in her short film, Mommy Books at a Mad Hatter Tea Party.

Author's Note

I created Dreadlocks and the Three Bears for my little boy (Kijana) because there were so few media images celebrating Black children. I first told this story in Dr. Wanna Zinsmaster's Storytelling for Teachers class (California State University-Los Angeles). I always dreamed of turning Dreadlocks and the Three Bears into a picture book. Unable to do so, my disappointment quickly disappeared when I observed my son's love of dissolve animation. I couldn't publish a picture book but I could and did make an award-winning Dreadlocks and the Three Bears dissolve animation video. When my son grew up, he became a multidisciplinary artist. As a producer, he brought together artists of different disciplines and generations including his friend (designer Simon Estrada), then combined my handcrafted collage-art with digital technology to make this picture book dream come true.